THE SCOTS AND SCOTCH-IRISH IN AMERICA

THE SCOTS AND SCOTCH-IRISH IN AMERICA

JAMES E. JOHNSON, Ph.D.

Associate Professor of History
Bethel College

Published by
Lerner Publications Company
Minneapolis, Minnesota

Second Printing 1967

Copyright © 1966 by Lerner Publications Company

International Copyright Secured. Printed in U.S.A.

Library of Congress Catalog Card Number: AC 66-10151

4

...CONTENTS...

Capturing the *Serapis.* When John Paul Jones was asked by the commander of the *Serapis* if he wanted to surrender, Jones cried, "I have not yet begun to fight."

Foreword

The Scots and Scotch-Irish in America is really the story of one people, those whose native land was Scotland. History, however, dealt in such a way with the Scottish people that they divided into two distinct groups.

The first group is composed of those Scots who lived in Scotland and came directly from their country to America. This story is told in Part I.

The second group is called the Scotch-Irish. They trace their existence to the emigration of Scots from Scotland to Northern Ireland, an area also known by the name Ulster. Many of the descendants of these people later immigrated to the American colonies. Their experiences had made them into a group with distinctive qualities. They were no longer just Scots, but neither had they become Irish. They were best described by coining a new word to cover their new character. They had become the Scotch-Irish, or as they are sometimes called, the Ulster Scots. The story of the Scotch-Irish in Ulster and their immigration to America is told in Parts II through VI. They are an important part of America's past, and their history had to be told separately to do them justice.

Parts VII and VIII give an account of the individuals of Scottish ancestry, including both the Scots and the Scotch-Irish, who have made an impact on American history.

PART I.

The Scots

1. *The Highlanders and the Lowlanders*

Scotland is divided into two sections: the Highlands and the Lowlands. The names describe the regions. One is high ground and mountainous: the other low lying, with lakes and plains. Almost two-thirds of the people of Scotland live in the central lowlands, although this area is only one-tenth of the entire country.

The Highlanders were originally warlike herdsmen who wore strange garments called kilts, and had won fame on the field of battle to the music of strange instruments called bagpipes. Their warriors were almost legendary, and poets and storytellers have told of their bravery. Highlanders were divided into groups called clans, each of which had distinctively patterned tartans, badges, and war cries. The main clans included such well-known names as the Campbells, MacLeans, MacKenzies, MacIntoshes, MacDonalds, and MacGregors. An insult or injury to any one of a clan was to be avenged by the entire community. Their devotion to their traditional dress continued even after they left Scotland. In June 1775, a man named Daniel McLeod petitioned the New York legislature, saying that some Highlanders recently arrived from Scotland would gladly serve under him in defense of the colony, "with the provision of having liberty to wear their own Country Dress commonly called the Highland Habit."

The basic reason for the emigration of the Scots, both Highlanders and Lowlanders, from their native land to America was poverty and hard times. The majority of the immigrants were forced to leave their country because of crop failures, low cattle prices, unemployment, and evictions from their farms. Stories had come back to them that in the New World there were no titled landlords to tyrannize the farmer, and that men were valued according to their abilities. They came to look upon America as a place of hope and promise, with cheap land, low taxes, high wages, and a healthy climate.

2. *The Migration to America*

Discharged soldiers from the Seven Years' War (1754-1761) between the British and the French and Indians were among the first Scottish settlers. Thousands of such soldiers stayed in America at the conclusion of the war and were given farms by the English government. These men wrote letters home which attracted others to come.

The discharged veterans saw a future for themselves in the colonies better than anything they could hope for back in the Highlands of Scotland. Overpopulation and unemployment had driven them into the army in the first place. Out of a group of 12,000 Highlanders who enlisted in the Seven Years' War only 76 returned to Scotland. They settled down on lands offered by a Royal Proclamation of October 7, 1763, on easy terms to officers and men who had served in the British forces. Most of them found homes in New York Province and Prince Edward Island.

In November 1767, another group landed at Brunswick, North Carolina. Governor Tryon granted them land in Cumberland and Mecklenburg counties, clear of all fees, at the rate of 100 acres per person, man, woman, or child. The largest family, a man, his wife, and four children, received a little more than their quota, a neat square mile, or 640 acres of land. Can you imagine the feelings of a man who received this much land free, even though it was virgin wilderness? In Scotland he had to maintain his family from the produce of only 10 or 12 acres.

Most of the Scottish emigrants who were attracted by the stories about America could obtain passage only by becoming indentured servants. An indentured servant was one who signed a contract agreeing to work for some person in America in return for payment of his passage over. The term of service was usually from four to seven years. At the end of that time they were free men and women, able to choose another way of life.

In March of 1774 a gentleman in Glasgow, writing to a friend in Philadelphia, said that, "the distress of the common people here is deeper and more general than you can imagine. There is an almost total stagnation in our manufactures, and grain is dear; many hundreds of labourers and mechanics, especially weavers in this neighbourhood, have lately indented and gone to America."

Shortly before his death in 1774, Sir William Johnson, the celebrated Indian Superintendent, induced many Highlanders to settle on his lands in the Mohawk Valley. Johnson built up a sort of private kingdom here. He was a good landlord, but he did compel his tenants, as had been done in the Highlands, to have their grain ground at his mill. These Scots were to form the backbone of Tory resistance to the Revolution in New York and to move to new homes in Glengary County, Ontario, because of their loyalty to England.

The English government became alarmed at the growing number of Scottish emigrants leaving for America. It feared that they might be infected with radical American principles and become at once a loss to the British army and a gain to the American. This possibility was the reason why emigration from Scotland was prohibited in 1775.

Others opposed emigration to America because of their fear that Scotland would lose too many skilled workers. Scottish newspapers contained advertisements from America calling for carpenters, blacksmiths, masons, and other artisans. Many colonies, especially in the South, had been offering inducements to prospective immigrants. Some colonies offered 50 acres of free land to every individual entering the area. Georgia encouraged Scottish settlers to come to their colony so that they might be settled on the frontier as a buffer against the Spanish and the Indians.

3. *The American Revolution and Its Consequences*

The coming of the American Revolution transformed Scotland's relations with America. The conservatism of the great majority of Scots in the colonies exposed them to increasing unpopularity and abuse from Americans. The Scottish emigrants from Ulster played a vigorous part in the Revolution, especially in Pennsylvania, where they promptly declared their allegiance to the patriot cause. The Scots from both the Highlands and Lowlands, however, remained loyal to the crown, maintaining a deep attachment to their country of origin. With a few exceptions, the Scots and Scotch-Irish were opposed to each other during the period of the Revolutionary War. They actually fought on opposite sides at the battle of King's Mountain in North Carolina. This engagement prevented Lord Cornwallis' attempt to organize a new regiment of North Carolina Highlanders for the British army.

Although we will not tell the full story of the Scottish contribution to American history at this point, it should be mentioned that

James Wilson, an outstanding statesman of the Revolutionary War period, emigrated from Scotland in 1765.

11

despite the British sympathies of the majority of the American Scots, they also contributed leaders and heroes to the Revolution. For example, two signers of the Declaration of Independence were born in Scotland, James Wilson, who had come from Carskerdo, Scotland, and John Witherspoon from Gifford, Scotland.

James Wilson was an attorney who became prominent in the affairs of Pennsylvania. He was a Pennsylvanian representative to the Constitutional Convention, and later appointed a justice of the first Supreme Court of the United States, where he served until his death in 1798. John Witherspoon was an educator and the president of Princeton University, which had been founded in 1746.

Patrick Henry, governor of Virginia, was also a Scot, and a fiery patriot. His famous words "give me liberty or give me death," are learned by every American. He was born in Hanover County, Virginia, but his father had emigrated to America from Aberdeen, Scotland. No colonial leader was more outspoken on behalf of independence from Great Britain.

Patrick Henry, an orator and politician. Henry's speeches inspired many to join the cause for independence.

John Paul Jones, painted by Charles Willson Peale. Jones came to America in 1775 and became a naval hero.

John Paul Jones was the leading naval hero of the Revolutionary War. He had been born in the parish of Kirkbeam in Kirkcudbrightshire, Scotland, and came to America at the beginning of the Revolution. The Continental Congress entrusted him with the command of several smaller ships. He cruised for some time off the coast of his native Scotland and captured some British merchantmen. In 1779 he was given command of a French ship which he renamed the *Bonhomme Richard* (Poor Richard) as a compliment to Benjamin Franklin. In September 1779, his vessel won in an engagement with the *Serapis,* a much larger English warship. Captain Pearson, commander of the *Serapis,* asked Jones if he was ready to give up, since the fight seemed to be going badly for the *Bonhomme Richard.* Jones gave the now-famous reply, "I've just begun to fight." There are two monuments to Captain Jones in this country, one at Annapolis, and one at Potomac Park in Washington.

After 1775, Scottish influence in America lost much of its force. The Scots who left America during and after the Revolution went to Florida, Halifax, Canada, and England. Bad harvests in the years 1782-83 caused a new burst of emigration but as a result of the Revolution, the stream of immigrants shifted from North Carolina and New York to the Canadian areas of Ontario, Nova Scotia (New Scotland), and Prince Edward Island.

Although Scottish emigration to America in the 18th century was on a small scale, their influence was greater than it has ever been since that time. The Scots then filled positions in political and administrative offices, in the professions, and in the field of commerce. The 19th century, on the other hand, saw a larger number of Scottish immigrants, but they became lost in the general immigration of the times, which grew steadily until almost one million people arrived in a single year. The greatest period of Scottish emigration to America was the decade of the 1920's. In these years the unemployed Lowlanders again faced hard times, and more than 300,000 of them came to the United States.

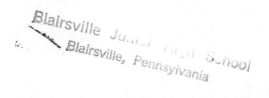

Had it not been for the American Revolution, the Scots might be as numerous in the United States as they are in Canada. The kilt and glengary might then be as familiar in Detroit, Michigan as they are in Windsor, Ontario, just across the United States-Canadian border.

4. *A Brief Glance at Prominent Scottish-Americans*

The last two chapters of this book are devoted to those persons of Scottish and Scotch-Irish descent who have achieved prominence in American life. This section will only glance at a few individuals of the last two centuries who were either born in Scotland or are of direct Scottish descent.

Gilbert Stuart, the great early American artist, was the son of an immigrant from Perth, Scotland. Stuart's work includes portraits of Presidents Washington, Adams, Jefferson, Madison, Monroe, and John Quincy Adams, Kings George III and IV of England, and

Gilbert Stuart, from a portrait by Charles Willson Peale and his son.

Herman Melville wrote *Moby Dick,* the story of a great white whale.

14

Louis XVII of France. He was considered the foremost portrait painter of his time.

Christopher (Kit) Carson was one of America's frontier heroes. He was born in Kentucky, but his grandfather, William Carson, was an immigrant from Scotland who had settled in North Carolina. Carson became a trapper, guide, Indian agent, and soldier. He first gained prominence by serving as Lt. John Charles Fremont's guide on Western expeditions, and later as an Indian fighter and soldier during the Mexican War.

Herman Melville, the author of one of America's literary classics, *Moby Dick,* was born in New York, but he is descended from a long line of Scots. His earliest known ancestor was Sir Richard de Melvill, who was forced, in 1296, to swear allegiance to King Edward I of England when he conquered Scotland. Melville went to sea at 18, and his books frequently tell of sea voyages and adventuring in remote places. His other works include the novels *Omoo, Typee, White Jacket,* and *Billy Budd.*

Alexander Bell, making the first telephone call between New York and Chicago in 1892.

Andrew Carnegie came to America in 1848. He became wealthy and gave millions of dollars to charity.

UNITED STATES POSTAGE

4¢

ANDREW CARNEGIE

Alexander Graham Bell, the inventor of the telephone and an outstanding figure in the education of the deaf, came to the United States from Edinburgh in 1870 at the age of 23. He created the telephone in 1876 and by April 3, 1877 was able to converse between Boston and New York. Bell never lost his love for his native Scotland and he purchased a large estate in Nova Scotia where he spent his summers. When he died on August 2, 1922, they buried him there on a mountain top in a tomb cut in the rock. Every telephone on the North American continent was silent during the burial service.

Andrew Carnegie, America's great steel manufacturer, was born at Dunferlime, Scotland, the son of a handloom weaver. The family came to America in 1848 and settled at Allegheny, Pennsylvania. Carnegie became the personal secretary and private telegrapher for Thomas Scott of the Pennsylvania Railroad, and so began the career which led him to build a huge industry, and become fabulously wealthy. Eventually he owned his own iron ore mines, coal mines, steamship lines, railroad lines, and steel mills. In 1900, the profits of the Carnegie Company were about 40 million dollars. Carnegie gave away about 350 million dollars before his death, much of this being in the form of libraries which he donated to cities, towns, and universities. He died in 1919 and was buried in Sleepy Hollow on the Hudson River.

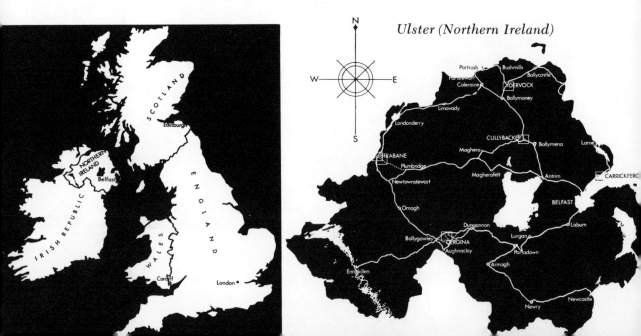

Ulster (Northern Ireland)

PART II.

The Scotch-Irish

1. *Ulster (Northern Ireland)*

Ulster is a portion of the northern section of the island of Ireland. In the center of Ulster lies the heart of the Scotch-Irish country, comprising the counties of Tyrone, Donegal, Londonderry, and Antrim. There are also the counties of Fermanagh, Monaghan, Armagh, Cavan, and Down. The latter is less than a dozen miles from Ayrshire in Scotland. How this part of Ireland was settled by the Scots is the subject of this chapter.

The Irish inhabitants of Ulster were in constant rebellion against the English kings and the advisors to King James I decided that peace could only be obtained by planting colonies of English and Scottish settlers among the Irish. King James, thereupon, decided to transform this section of Catholic Ireland into a Protestant stronghold. He set about to do this by confiscating the lands of the native chiefs in Ulster and bestowing them upon English and Scottish lords on condition they settle the territory with tenants from Scotland and England. This is sometimes called the "great settlement" and it marks the beginning of the transformation of Ulster into a Protestant territory.

The term Scotch-Irish does not refer to a racial mixture. The Ulster settlers who came from Scotland did not mix with the native Irish to any great extent. The religious barrier, among other things, prevented this since the newcomers were mostly Presbyterians and the natives were Irish Roman Catholic. A common saying reported among the older settlers was "We're not Eerish bot Scoatch."

Even before the Ulster settlement scheme of King James began, there was already a considerable Scottish occupation of the region nearest to Scotland. The advisors to the king had hoped that the new settlers in Ulster would be mostly English, but it was soon evident that the Scottish Lowlanders were better equipped to endure the hardships of resettlement.

No census figures are available, but it has been estimated that there were some 100,000 Scots and only 20,000 English living in Ulster by the middle of the 17th century. The Scotch-Irish became the backbone of the business people in Ulster. They were especially important in founding the weaving and milling industries.

2. *Economic Pressure and Political Persecution*

The Glorious Revolution of 1688 which resulted in the expulsion of James II from the English throne caused little violence in England. Ireland, however, experienced a bloody civil war since the greater part of that country remained loyal to James II. The Ulster Presbyterians were prompt to declare their allegiance to the new English rulers William and Mary, and Presbyterian ministers took the lead in organizing the people for defense against the followers of James. Ireland, outside of Ulster, was in the hands of Tyrconnel, the deputy of James, and Tyrconnel moved quickly to force Ulster to submit. The Protestants of Ulster, however, made heroic stands at Enniskillen and Londonderry and Tyrconnel was held back. In 1690 William of Orange, whose position in England was now secure, sent troops to Ireland and administered a crushing defeat to the forces of James at the battle of Boyne.

This was followed by a further confiscation of Irish lands and by the Williamite settlement, by which the Irish Catholics lost an additional million and a half acres of land. Scottish migration to Ulster increased in tempo as a result of these events since land was now offered on very generous terms. It has been estimated that 50,000 Scots arrived in Ulster between the years 1690-1697.

The years of the 18th century, however, were to be characterized by a steady stream of Scotch-Irish out of Ulster to other parts of the world. There were various reasons for this migration, the most important being economic pressures and religious persecution. The Irish woolen trade had been shut out of Scotland, England, and America, but the British woolen industry still protested its existence. As a result, the British Parliament in 1699 completed the exclusion by prohibiting the Irish from exporting manufactured wool "to any other country whatever." In 1717-18, many farmers were evicted when they refused, or were unable, to pay higher rents to their English landlords.

After these experiences, the Scotch-Irish of Ulster, bitter against England, sought a country where they might have free land and self-government. It has been estimated that over 4,000 left for America in 1718. After the famine of 1740, more than 12,000 left annually. In the half century before the American Revolution, perhaps 200,000 persons, or one-third of the Protestant population of Ulster, emigrated, the majority going to America.

In Ireland it was feared that the whole country would be depopulated, especially of its more skilled inhabitants. Archbishop Boulter, Lord Primate of All Ireland, writing in 1728, said: "The whole north is in a ferment at present, and people every day engaging one another to go. . . . The worst is, that it affects only Protestants, and reigns chiefly in the north, which is the seat of our linen manufacture." The combination of economic oppression and famine, the latter notably in the years 1727 and 1740, thus caused many thousands to flee from Ulster with the hope of a better life in some other land.

Another significant factor in the emigration of the Scotch-Irish from Ulster was that of religious persecution. The Church of England had been declared the Established Church of Ireland. The Scotch-Irish, however, were Presbyterians and their growth and prosperity soon caused a series of laws to be passed intended to make them conform to the Established Church.

The Test Act of 1704, enacted by the Parliament under Queen Anne, was a blow against Protestant dissenters, in general, and against Ulster Presbyterians, in particular. This act excluded them from all civil and military offices under the crown by requiring all who served in these capacities to take communion of the Established Church.

The stream of emigration slackened after the first impact of the Test Act, perhaps in the hope that the law would be changed. When that hope ended, men of spirit and energy refused to remain in a country where they were held unfit to enjoy the privileges of citizenship. Consequently, until this condition was changed in 1782, shipload after shipload of emigrants departed from Belfast and Londonderry. They carried a deep resentment in their hearts against the British, which showed itself when the opportunity arose. In the American War for Independence, England found staunch opposition from the grandsons and great-grandsons of the Presbyterians who had been driven from Ulster by the Test Act.

The religious persecution of the Presbyterians in Ulster was a blunder. If the leaders of the Established Church had treated them with more tact, they probably would have been less willing to brave the dangers of an ocean crossing. The economic hardships of the times might not have driven the Scotch-Irish to emigration, if religious discrimination had not also been present. An Ulster Scot might starve at home but he could not tolerate any meddling with his views of right and wrong and eternal destiny.

3. *Difficulties at Sea*

The emigrants who left Ulster were subjected to the usual dangers of an ocean crossing during this period of history. The ships were often unsafe for such a journey and usually very overcrowded. Seldom was enough water taken for the entire voyage, and what there was often stank. Most people took a keg of vinegar with them to add to the water before drinking. The food often became moldy and rotten and totally unfit for human consumption.

Sickness and disease were all too common. Dysentery was a constant danger. The dreaded "ship's fever" usually meant an outbreak of cholera and almost daily burials at sea. Storms at sea made life particularly miserable for the passengers since they were then confined below deck for long periods of time. Many of them had only straw for beds and when this became damp and moldy it had to be thrown overboard.

One especially terrible story was that of the *Seaflower* which sailed from Belfast, Ireland on July 10, 1741, bound for Philadelphia. There were 106 persons aboard. They had barely begun the voyage when the captain died and the first mate was taken ill. The ship sprung her mast, was unable to navigate properly, and provisions ran low. In order to stay alive, the living began to eat the dead. After six bodies had been cut up and eaten, the *Success*, a man-of-war, came along and supplied them with food for the rest of the trip. By the time the voyage ended on October 31, 46 people had died.

In addition to the difficulties of food, water, accommodations, and storms there was always the problem of fights breaking out, because people were too closely confined. These were the hardships which immigrants were willing to endure, however, in the hope that their new life in America would make it all worthwhile.

PART III.

Scotch-Irish Settlements in America

1. *New England*

There was a mutual bond between the English Puritans living in Ulster and the Scotch Presbyterians. They both opposed the Established Church of England and felt oppressed by its policies. For this reason some of the early Scotch-Irish emigrants headed for New England.

In the period from 1714 to 1720 inclusive, about 54 vessels arrived in Boston from Ireland, most of them from Ulster. The Puritans were eager to settle the Scotch-Irish on the frontier where they could serve as a first line of defense against the Indians. The Surveyor-General of Customs at Boston, Thomas Lechmere, wrote in 1718 that the Scotch-Irish "are come over hither for no other reason but upon encouragement sent from hence . . . that they should have so many acres of land given them gratis to settle our frontiers as a barrier against the Indians."

The Scotch-Irish settlers constituted the border garrisons and bore the brunt of any Indian uprisings. Their Ulster training had prepared them for such hardships, however, and their settlement on the frontiers marks the beginning of a period of expansion into new territory.

The Puritans of New England were generally hostile to outsiders, however, and the Scotch-Irish were soon no exception to this rule. A Scotch-Irish settlement at Worcester, Massachusetts, was destroyed by a mob at night. Cotton Mather, one of the most famous ministers in the Massachusetts Bay Colony, opposed the plans for allowing Scotch-Irish settlements on the frontier as "formidable attempts of Satan and his Sons to Unsettle us." Eventually most of the Scotch-Irish at Worcester moved to Pelham, farther west. The Scotch-Irish arrivals in Boston were usually hurried out of the city as fast as possible. The excuses given were many, but as one official wrote in 1718, "these confounded Irish will eat us all up, provisions being most extravagently dear and scarce of all sorts."

One group of settlers who arrived in Boston in August 1718, chose a place on the frontier called Nutfield. The abundance of chestnut, walnut, and butternut trees in the forest gave the site its name. The settlers named the place Londonderry in honor of the city in Ulster which had been made famous by the bravery of their fathers. By 1734, according to church records, there were 700 people who attended communion to receive the sacrament. Londonderry, New Hampshire, became a thriving community with the culture of flax and potatoes as well as the home manufacture of linen. The McClellands, Campbells, McDonalds, McGregors, McNeils, Magills, and Fergusons were among the prominent families of this American Londonderry.

The New England colonies would probably have become the chosen home of most Ulster immigrants, but their mixed reception and experiences were such that the stream of Ulster settlers turned farther south. Although there were over 500 Scotch-Irish settlements in America at the time of the Revolution, only 70 were in New England. The Scotch-Irish taught their Puritan neighbors the value of the potato as an article of food and laid the foundation for a spinning and weaving industry. The roll call of famous Scotch-Irish settlers in New England is quite impressive and includes

John Stark served as an officer in both the French and Indian War and the Revolutionary War.

Henry Knox was an outstanding soldier of the Revolutionary War and one of Washington's most trusted advisors.

General John Stark and General Henry Knox of the Revolutionary War. Other colonies, however, offered attractive opportunities, and the Scotch-Irish were not slow to take advantage of them and move on.

2. *Pennsylvania*

The Susquehanna and Delaware River Valleys

Pennsylvania became the favorite colony of Scotch-Irish settlers. The reports which filtered back to Ulster regarding Pennsylvania were usually excellent. The liberal laws, low taxes, and political, economic, social, and religious freedom were most appealing. Only in Rhode Island was liberty offered on such terms as these, but Rhode Island was a limited area and had been settled before, and the land in Rhode Island was not as fertile as that of Pennsylvania. The cold reception which the Scotch-Irish had received in Massachusetts caused them to turn away from New England. All in all, Pennsylvania appeared to be the home which the Scotch-Irish had long been seeking.

The Scotch-Irish began to arrive in Pennsylvania in great numbers and caused James Logan, the Secretary of Pennsylvania Province, to write in 1727 that "we have from the North of Ireland great numbers . . . eight or nine ships . . . discharged at Newcastle." He later added, "It looks as if Ireland is to send all its inhabitants hither, for last week not less than six ships arrived, and every day, two or three arrive also."

The early settlers in Pennsylvania moved up the river valleys, particularly those of the Susquehanna and Delaware Rivers. The Scotch-Irish settlers flowed around the Quaker settlements and into the back country. They set up their cabins, their mills, and their Presbyterian churches. They were usually the less permanent settlers, and frequently sold out their clearings to a second wave of immigrants who further developed the work which they had started. The Susquehanna and Cumberland Valleys became strongholds of Scotch-Irish influence. Such towns as Chambersburg, Gettysburg, Carlisle, and York still contain numbers of the descendants of the early Scotch-Irish pioneers.

The Scotch-Irish settlers in Pennsylvania became the typical western "squatters," that is, they looked for free land and then settled on it without asking the permission of anyone. Secretary Logan of Pennsylvania wrote in 1730 that the Scotch-Irish had settled on Conestoga Manor, a tract of 15,000 acres which the Penn family had reserved for themselves. Logan stated that he did not know how to get these people off the land since they stated it was "against the laws of God and nature that so much land should be idle when so many Christians wanted it to labor on. . . ." The usefulness of the Scotch-Irish as a shield against Indian attacks was early recognized by Secretary Logan. He wrote a letter in 1729 explaining how and why he intended to use the Scotch-Irish settlers:

> About this time [1720] a considerable number of people came in from Ireland who wanted to be settled, at the same time it happened that we were under the same apprehensions from northern Indians. . . . I therefore thought it might be prudent to plant a settlement of fresh men as those who formerly had so bravely defended Inniskillen and Derry as a frontier in case of any disturbance.

An Indian attack on a frontier settlement in Tennessee. The Scotch-Irish were encouraged to settle on the frontier and serve as a shield against Indian attacks. They did not seem to mind, however, since land was cheap and they wished to be as far as possible from any established government.

The Scotch-Irish hated to pay any rent, however small. This can be simply explained by their experience in Ulster, where rents had been raised after they had settled in the country and made the land valuable by their hard work. Secretary Logan wrote in 1730 that the "settlement of five families from Ireland gives me more trouble than 50 of any other people." Later, the Scotch-Irish were to be charged with provoking Indian outbreaks and with the massacre of friendly Indians.

Western Pennsylvania

The Scotch-Irish usually landed at Philadelphia and proceeded to the interior to find a place to settle. They arrived in such great numbers that Secretary Logan expressed the fear that "they will make themselves proprietor of the province." By 1730, Pennsylvania had its Derry, Donegal, Tyrone, and Coleraine townships. There was a Toboyne in Derry County, and a Fermanagh Township in Juanita County, as well as an Ulster and a Chester County.

The Donegal, Paxtany, Derry, and Hanover townships, together with some lands north of Wilmington, and also the Allen township west of Easton, comprise the earliest Scotch-Irish settlements in Pennsylvania.

The Scotch-Irish settlements in Lancaster, Lebanon, Dauphin, and York counties were located in a region which was rapidly being colonized by German settlers. The Scotch-Irish soon found themselves surrounded by unfamiliar neighbors. Disagreements and disturbances of various kinds arose between the two groups. As a result, the Penn family instructed their agents in 1743 to sell no lands in this region to the Scotch-Irish, but to make them generous offers if they would move to the Cumberland Valley farther to the west. Many of the Scotch-Irish settlers accepted this offer to move west and sold out to German settlers. The Germans were much better farmers than the Scotch-Irish, taking time to remove the stumps and improve the land. By 1749, it was estimated that the Scotch-Irish composed about one-fourth of the whole population of Pennsylvania.

A forest clearing. After clearing the land and building a home in the forest, the Scotch-Irish often sold their plots to more permanent settlers and moved farther westward.

There were at least four reasons why the Scotch-Irish settled on the frontiers in America. First, land was cheap out on the frontier and large families could be supported with little expense. Second, the government encouraged them to settle the frontier as a shield against Indian attacks. Third, they wanted to be as far away as possible from any established civil authority for they were suspicious of government. Fourth, they wanted to be where they would have complete religious liberty to worship in any manner they chose.

The first phase of Scotch-Irish settlement in Pennsylvania dealt with the areas just described. In the region east of the Susquehanna River they were outnumbered by both the English and the Germans; west of the Susquehanna, as far as the Allegheny Mountains, they were the most numerous national group. Western Pennsylvania became a distinct section, occupied predominantly by Scotch-Irish, a fact which was to have an important effect upon the internal politics of that province.

3. *Conflict Between the Quakers and the Scotch-Irish*

The Scotch-Irish became involved in Pennsylvania politics at a very early date, but especially from the time of the French and Indian War. The issues of that war formed them into a political party which opposed the established leaders. From the beginning they came into conflict with the Quaker government, and the period from 1755 to 1776 is one of frequent clashes between the two groups.

The first serious clash took place over the question of military preparedness and was brought to a head by the French and Indian War. Following the defeat of General Braddock, the Indians attacked settlers in western Pennsylvania, burning homes and killing the inhabitants. The people requested help from the Quaker Assembly, but nothing was done to assist them.

The Quakers were devoted to "quietism" in religion and believed in non-violence. The Scotch-Irish, on the other hand, were willing to fight to protect their frontier homes. The peaceful Quakers opposed war with anyone, including the Indians, while the Scotch-Irishmen, who had always been exposed to the dangers of an Indian attack, regarded the Indians as enemies. The frontiersmen also resented the political monopoly of the eastern counties in the government of Pennsylvania. Again and again, the Quaker Assembly refused to give attention to the appeals for help and munitions to deal with the Indian menace. This exasperated the Scotch-Irish in western Pennsylvania, but even more upsetting was the fact that legally they could do nothing about it. In 1755 the Pennsylvania Assembly contained 36 members, and the Quakers numbered 26 of the entire group. This is significant since the Quakers consisted of only one-fifth of the population of the colony.

As matters became worse the Scotch-Irish took action. The Quakers were overthrown and steps taken to protect the frontier. Forts were erected and measures were adopted to supply men and money for defense. Voluntary bands of frontiersmen, known as rangers, were organized, whose responsibilities included manning the forts, and pursuing Indians seen in the vicinity of a settled community.

The Scotch-Irish had adopted the slogan that "the only good Indian was a dead one," and they even attacked a group of peaceful, Christianized Indians near Bethlehem and Lancaster who offered no resistance to them. The frontier settlers continued to denounce the Assembly in Philadelphia for inaction and finally a group of residents from the townships of Lebanon, Paxton, and Hanover decided to march on Philadelphia. This group, known as the "Paxton Boys," threatened to kill the Moravian Indians harbored in Philadelphia and to sack the town. The Moravian Indians were those who had been converted to Christianity by the German settlers, and were being protected from the frontiersmen, who viewed all Indians as enemies. General Gage and a company of British soldiers had to be brought in to guard the Indians. In the end, a conference was held just outside the city of Philadelphia and a settlement reached. Benjamin Franklin was one of the commissioners sent out by the city of Philadelphia. The "Paxton Boys" had demanded removal of the Indians from the colony, a return of prisoners held by the Indians, a reapportionment of the Assembly to give the western frontier counties an equal voice, and a bounty on Indian scalps. The conclusion of the matter was that the governor granted only their last demand.

4. *Maryland, Virginia, the Carolinas, and New York*

The Scotch-Irish settlers in Maryland, Virginia, and the Carolinas had usually settled first in Pennsylvania and then moved southward. The reasons for this were the inadequate protection they received from authorities in Pennsylvania against Indian raids, the mountain barriers to further westward expansion, and the cheapness of land farther south. It was simpler to follow the valleys going south than to penetrate the mountains to the west. As to the cheapness of land, it could be secured in Maryland and Virginia for one-third what it cost in Pennsylvania.

The Scotch-Irish found that it was easier to move to a new farm than to improve the existing one. They could not compete with the Germans in Pennsylvania when it came to farming and it was a natural process for a Scotch-Irishman to sell his undeveloped farm to a German immigrant and seek new land. This movement south was in its early stages when Robert Harper, a Scotch-Irishman, settled at the junction of the Shenandoah and Potomac Rivers in

Advertisement for land in the western part of Virginia. Many Scotch-Irish settlers in Pennsylvania eventually moved southward where land was cheaper.

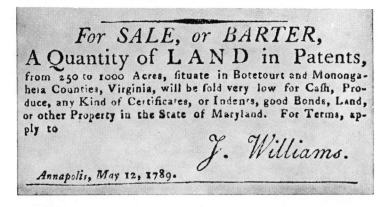

For SALE, or BARTER,
A Quantity of LAND in Patents, from 250 to 1000 Acres, situate in Botetourt and Mononga-heia Counties, Virginia, will be sold very low for Cash, Produce, any Kind of Certificates, or Indents, good Bonds, Land, or other Property in the State of Maryland. For Terms, apply to

J. Williams.

Annapolis, May 12, 1789.

1734 and founded Harper's Ferry. As they moved down the Shenandoah Valley, the Scotch-Irish founded the towns of Staunton, Lexington, and Fincastle. There are few places in America where the Scotch-Irish influence is more clearly seen than in Augusta and Roclabridge counties in Virginia. The Scotch-Irish are credited with the founding of Washington and Lee University in that area, and, at the same time, establishing it as one of the strongholds of Presbyterianism.

Many of the Scotch-Irish settlers in the Carolinas were those who had moved into the Shenandoah Valley of Virginia, and after a short stay there, decided to move on farther south. They settled in large numbers in the North Carolina counties of Granville, Orange, Rowan, Mecklenburg, Guilford, Davidson, and others. The Scotch-Irish established many schools and churches in North Carolina. They spread the Presbyterian religion throughout the province and were mainly responsible for establishing Davidson College. There were some Scotch-Irishmen who pushed even farther south into the piedmont country of South Carolina, among whom were the ancestors of John C. Calhoun.

The state of Kentucky was influenced by Pennsylvania Scotch-Irish settlers who moved down the Shenandoah Valley of Virginia. From there they proceeded to western North Carolina and then on the Wilderness Road across the mountains into Kentucky. Others moved into western Pennsylvania and then on into Ohio where they influenced the history of that state.

It was not until the great wave of Ulster emigration in 1718 that New York and New Jersey felt the impact of the Scotch-Irish. In 1720, settlers in the vicinity of Goshen, Orange County, New York were numerous enough to form a Presbyterian congregation. In the succeeding decade some 40 families from the north of Ireland settled in the country west of the Hudson in what became Orange and Ulster counties.

One of the influential settlers in New York was Robert Livingston, who moved there from Massachusetts in 1674. He obtained employment as a clerk to the Board of Commissioners, which then governed the Albany district, and began a prosperous official career in the course of which he acquired an extensive tract of land still known as the Livingston Manor. A town by that name still exists in southern New York State. There were other Scotch-Irish settlements in New York State, one of the most famous arising on a tract of land on Otsego County in a township known as Cherry Valley. By 1765 there were about 40 families located in Cherry Valley. At the time of the Revolution it was still very much a frontier settlement and contained only 60 families.

On October 11, 1778, Cherry Valley was attacked by the Tories and Indians, led by Walter Butler and Joseph Brant, the Mohawk chieftain. Thirty-two of the inhabitants, mostly women and children, were massacred as well as 16 Continental Army soldiers. The remainder of the inhabitants were carried off as prisoners and the buildings were burned. For seven years the site remained as a desolate reminder of the tragedy. It was not until about 1785 that some of the survivors began to return and rebuild the settlement.

A frontiersman guarding a settlement. The Scotch-Irish immigrants on the frontier were usually rugged fighters because of their experiences in Ulster.

PART IV.

The Presbyterian Church

1. *The Circuit Rider*

One of the permanent Scotch-Irish contributions to American culture was the Presbyterian Church. By 1776, each of the approximately 500 Scotch-Irish communities in America had at least one Presbyterian Church, and they extended from the New England frontier to Georgia.

The Scotch-Irish Presbyterian preacher followed close behind the first settlers and often led his congregation to a new home in the wilderness. He usually knew how to use a rifle and a plow, and was as much at home fighting Indians or felling a tree with an axe as he was preaching from the pulpit. These men were frequently powerful orators and many of them were scholars. Whenever a church was founded, the next thought of the preacher was to get a school started, and eventually perhaps a college. They were stern in their insistence that the young people learn the catechism.

Many of the preachers rode far afield in order that they might minister to their flock. They frequently rode what became known as "the Circuit." That is, they left home in order to visit the isolated settlements which had no church, and they might not return again for weeks or months. The circuit riders braved all kinds of weather and slept wherever they could when night arrived. Even though these men had to undergo severe physical hardship and received little pay for doing so, they had to pass difficult examinations in order that they might be licensed to preach. The founders of Presbyterianism made certain that their ministers were men of good training and sound learning.

2. *The Church in the Community*

The Presbyterian Church became a powerful force in the Scotch-Irish frontier communities. Men in the communities were apt to be restless, and impatient with any restraints, and on numerous occasions the civil authorities appealed to the Presbyterian pastors to help them maintain law and order. The Scotch-Irish frontiersman was a rough and unruly individual but he brought civilization to the wilderness through his churches and schools.

The first Presbyterian church in Pennsylvania, and perhaps in the nation, had its origin in the missionary labors of Francis Makemie, a Scotch-Irishman from County Donegal, Ireland. Makemie visited Philadelphia in 1692 and gathered a congregation of Presbyterians who, in 1698, formed the First Presbyterian Church of Philadelphia under Reverend Jedekiah Andrews. In population and position, Philadelphia was then more like a national capital than any other town in the colonies. Almost all of the great organizers of American Presbyterianism were connected with the Philadelphia Presbytery.

One interesting indication of the Scotch-Irish influence on the Presbyterian Church is in the names given to the presbyteries. The first New England Presbytery was organized about 1729 and named Londonderry. In 1732 Donegal Presbytery and in 1765 Carlisle Presbytery, both in Pennsylvania, were founded.

The Scotch-Irish Presbyterians took their religion very seriously. Families would often travel many miles under very difficult circumstances in order to attend church on the Sabbath day. The splits between Presbyterians, although they seemed trivial to outsiders, were often very serious to the individuals involved. One observer in western Pennsylvania reported that a man there had lived with his wife for more than 50 years but never attended her church, nor did she attend his. They were both Presbyterians, but when they reached a certain fork in the road each Sabbath day, she took their daughters to her church, and he took their sons to his church. The typical Scotch-Irishman often seemed to care little about where he stood with men, but was greatly concerned about his relationship with God.

3. *The Church and Education*

The Scotch-Irish in Ulster had always enjoyed an educated ministry because it was comparatively easy for a student to go to Scotland for training. A candidate for the ministry in Ulster would

A Circuit Rider, or traveling Presbyterian minister, braved bad weather and other hardships to preach to scattered Scotch and Scotch-Irish settlements.

receive a good education. Educated ministers, therefore, accompanied the Scotch-Irish immigrants from Ulster. The story in America was far different. There were no training centers here. If American-born Presbyterians were to become well educated, then institutions of learning would have to be set up. It was a situation similar to this which impelled the New England Puritans to found Harvard University in order to train their religious leaders.

In 1716 William Tennent, an Ulster clergyman and graduate of Edinburgh, emigrated to America. He applied to the Synod of Philadelphia and accepted a position at a church in Neshaming, Pennsylvania. James Logan gave Tennent 50 acres of land on Neshaming Creek, and Tennent put up a school house on the site. This school became known as the Log College. Log College made a substantial contribution to intellectual life in America. Among its pupils were Samuel Blair, James McCrea, John Blair, and Samuel Finley. The Tennent family, many of whom became Presbyterian ministers, were responsible for the spread of Presbyterianism in colonial America.

Many of the Presbyterian pastors founded classical schools known as academies and this gave opportunities to the young peo-

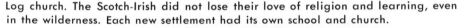

Log church. The Scotch-Irish did not lose their love of religion and learning, even in the wilderness. Each new settlement had its own school and church.

ple in their congregation who aimed at a higher education. At the same time, the clergy would put on the conscience of their people the duty of dedicating the choicest of their sons to the ministry of the gospel. It was a rather accepted thing among some families that at least one son would become a minister.

The Scotch-Irish Presbyterians were the first religious group to found institutions of higher learning in Pennsylvania. Since they were particularly numerous in the Cumberland Valley, they established Dickinson College at Carlisle, the first denominational school in Pennsylvania, and the twelfth college to be founded in the United States. Washington and Jefferson College in western Pennsylvania was also a Scotch-Irish institution. Other institutions in which Scotch-Irish Presbyterians have been influential are Allegheny College, Waynesburg College, Westminster College, and Geneva College, all of which are in Pennsylvania. They also had a part in the establishment of Transylvania College and Centre College in Kentucky, and Wooster College in Ohio.

The most significant contributions which the Scotch-Irish Presbyterians made to higher education in colonial America was Princeton College. Princeton was established in 1746, but began its most vigorous period of growth when Dr. John Witherspoon came over from Scotland to direct its affairs. Princeton graduated 230 students from 1766 to 1773, and from this group emerged 12 members of the Continental Congress, 24 members of the Congress of the United States, three justices of the Supreme Court, five cabinet members, one President, and one Vice-President. Nine members of the Constitutional Convention in 1787 were Princeton men. The influence of Princeton in the establishment of other educational institutions was also important. One of these was Hampden Sydney College in Virginia. It was founded in 1774, with the active support and approval of the Hanover Presbytery, and the site was fixed in Prince Edward County at a point convenient for the Scotch-Irish settlements in Virginia and North Carolina. The first president of the college, The Reverend Stanhope Smith, was a Princeton graduate.

PART V.

Everyday Life in a Scotch-Irish Settlement

1. *Clearing the Land*

The Scotch-Irish settled first in colonies because this afforded security against Indian attacks and enabled them to establish churches and schools. The typical Scotch-Irishman was too restless to stay in a settled community, however, and as soon as the danger from the Indians lessened he headed for the frontier.

The process by which the Scotch-Irish, and most frontier farmers, cleared the land was interesting. They usually selected a site where the woods were very thick, believing that this kind of soil was the most fertile. After all, if trees could grow there, why shouldn't crops do well? Then they would "girdle" the trees in a selected area. That is, they would cut a strip of bark from around the tree and kill it. When this was completed, they would cut down a number of trees to be used in building a cabin.

If the farmer settled in a very remote area, he had to depend on his family entirely for help in this work. If there were neighbors nearby they would hold a "logging bee" and a house raising. All would gather at a stated time and help their new neighbor erect his cabin. If enough help was available, this could be done in one or two days.

Cabin in the wilderness. The Scotch-Irish were often the settlers who built the first primitive cabins on the frontier.

Frontier farm. After several years of hard work, frontier settlers usually enlarged their clearings and built rough fences and shelters for their animals.

The trees which had been "girdled" would lose their leaves and the first crop of corn was often planted among the dead and dying trees. The next year the trees might be felled and burned, and then the corn crop would be planted among the stumps. The job of removing these stumps often fell to the patient German settler who bought the farm when the Scotch-Irishman moved farther west. The animals were usually allowed to roam in the woods at first. Later on, crude fencing and some rough out buildings might be erected to give the pigs, cows, and sheep some protection from the weather and the wild animals.

The Scotch-Irish settler labored under some very serious disadvantages. One of the worst was his difficulty in getting his crops to market. Western Pennsylvania farmers had to send their goods by pack train over the mountains to Philadelphia or by flat boat down the rivers to New Orleans. Both routes were long and the dangers from Indians and thieves were very great. He also faced the problem of Indian raids, loss of his animals to snakes and wild beasts, and the probability that a good portion of his crops would be devoured by squirrels from the surrounding forests.

2. *Family Life*

The pioneer farmer had to be a jack-of-all-trades in order to survive. All members of the family shared in the tasks of domestic manufacturing. The spinning and weaving of flax and wool for clothing and other uses was an art which the Scotch-Irish brought over with them from Ulster. In addition, the frontier family had to make furniture, shoes, candles, soap, maple sugar, and home preserved foods. The drying of fruits and vegetables was very important if the family was to survive during the long months of winter. Later on, as more settlers moved into an area, there arrived on the scene such craftsmen as the village shoemaker, saddler, blacksmith, cooper, and other craftsmen.

The life of a woman in a frontier household was very hard indeed. A woman had to do the family cooking, washing, and sewing. She broke and carded flax, spun and wove the cloth, and then made clothing and bedding for the family. She also milked the cows, churned butter, tended the poultry, worked in the garden, roamed the woods in search of nuts, berries, and herbs, and dried the fruits for winter use. She made the jams, jellies, pickles, and preserves for the family, assisted in the fields during the harvest season, cared for the sick, instructed her children, and learned to use a gun to defend the home when her husband was away. There were no cookstoves, (the cooking was done over an open fireplace), laundries, or running water in the house. Everything had to be done the hard way, and women often died at a very early age.

The customary foods of a Scotch-Irish household would be fried mush with wild honey, pone bread, succotash, johnny-cake, hominy, potatoes, and turnips. A popular dish was hog and hominy, and it should be noted that they used corn in a great many ways. Practically every Scotch-Irishman knew how to use a gun and relied on deer, bear, rabbits, squirrels, turkeys, ducks, and pigeons for meat. Fish from the nearby streams and lakes provided some variety in the diet. Sweets consisted of maple sugar, wild honey, and molasses. One Scotch-Irishman wrote to his sister in Ulster urging her to come to America. He described the abundance of food to be enjoyed by saying, "as for chestnuts, walnuts, hazel nuts, strawberries, blackberries, and mulberries, they grow wild in the field,

Neighbors gathered to separate flax. The Scotch-Irish settlers helped each other with many tasks, turning work projects into social events.

A stockade was a necessary part of life on the frontier. Families on scattered farms fled to stockades when they were warned of Indian raids.

and woods in vast quantities." Another person described the wealth of food in America in this way: "I believe I saw more peaches and apples rotting on the ground than would sink the British fleet. I was at many plantations in Ohio where they no more knew the number of their hogs than myself . . . The poorest families adorn the table three times a day like a wedding dinner — tea, coffee, beef, fowls, pies, eggs, pickles, good bread . . ."

3. *Social Life and Defense*

The amusements which the Scotch-Irish enjoyed were plain and simple. Their social events often had a practical purpose to serve, such as a house raising, flax pulling, corn husking, or a quilting party. A visit to a neighbor's farm several miles away was quite an occasion. Dancing was regarded as a primary form of entertainment for young and old alike. The muster of the militia was a signal for a time of eating and drinking and games. The men would use their famous "long rifles" to shoot at targets and compete for prizes.

Weddings were events of unusual interest in the social life of the Scotch-Irish pioneers. On the morning of the wedding day the men gathered at the house of the bride and selected two of their number to "run for the bottle." These two men would race ahead until the party of the groom was sighted, and the first to reach them was named the winner and returned with a bottle of spirits to begin the day's festivities. The wedding ceremony was followed by a very large dinner and then dancing until late in the evening. A house raising for the newly married couple was usually held soon after the wedding. "Wakes" were also common among the Scotch-Irish, that is, the neighbors came to a home where a member of the family had died and sat up all night with them. During the night the people would do a great deal of eating and drinking. In the morning, the neighbors would then dig a grave and assist the family in the burial.

The Scotch-Irish looked for usefulness in all things since they had to struggle constantly to survive. They did not try to trim any of the shrubbery growing near their cabin for it would serve no practical purpose. They saw small need for shoes in the summer if the soles of their feet were tough. The hunting shirt worn by most of the men was a kind of loose frock with the bosom sewed as a wallet in which they placed bread, cakes, or dried venison, as well as a rag for wiping their rifle barrel.

Their forts consisted of cabins, blockhouses, and stockades. A large folding gate made of thick slabs of wood closed the fort. Such places might appear trifling when compared to the strong military posts of Europe and America, but they served their purpose. Any family awakened at night and told of the presence of raiding Indians would go to the fort with the utmost haste. No sounds were made, for everyone knew, including the young children, that they were in great danger. Since the Indians had no artillery they seldom took these forts, although the individual farms were often raided and the inhabitants killed before they could flee to the fort.

Such were the living conditions of the Scotch-Irish on the frontier of America. They were used to hardships because of their Ulster experiences, and the abundance of land and game in America offered the hope of a better life than they had known. That they took to the backwoods life with relish is shown by their eagerness to move on west whenever the opportunity to do so arose. A tombstone over the grave of a Scotch-Irish pioneer in the Shenandoah Valley presents a brief but vivid picture of the history of this group:

Here lies the remains of John Lewis, who slew the Irish lord, settled in Augusta County, located the town of Staunton, and furnished five sons to fight the battles of the American Revolution.

PART VI.

The Scotch-Irish in the American Revolution

1. *Their Resentment Against England*

The province of Ulster and the American colonies had common interests in the 18th century. Both were dependencies of the British crown and both resented the efforts of Parliament to govern them and, particularly, to tax them. The active part which the Scotch-Irish took in the American Revolution was a continuation of the resistance to British policy that began in Ulster. The Scotch-Irish had left Ulster because of oppressions which they could not bear, and they would not tolerate the idea that these oppressions should now follow them to America. They did not want to have their freedoms or their religious liberty tampered with once they were in America. For these reasons they furnished much of the manpower of the Continental Army to see that this did not happen.

It would be logical to assume that the Scotch-Irish living out on the remote frontier would not be affected by the revolutionary ideas on the east coast of America. This was not the case, however, and the frontier people often demonstrated a zeal to oppose England that went beyond what could be found on the coast. When the British closed the port of Boston in retaliation for the Boston Tea Party, a meeting was held in Carlisle, Pennsylvania, soon after, condemning the British action. They chose deputies to be sent to a provincial convention, and among them was James Wilson, who had been born in Scotland and was a signer of the Declaration of Independence. Thomas Polk, a great uncle of President Polk, read a "Mecklenburg Declaration" in North Carolina in 1775, and it expresses the sentiment of the Scotch-Irish settlers in America towards British policy: "Resolved, that whosoever ... countenanced the unchartered and dangerous invasion of our rights, as claimed by Great Britain, is an enemy to this county — to America — and to the inherent and inalienable rights of man."

2. *Their Military Contribution*

One of the Scotch-Irish who contributed a great deal to the cause of revolution was John Stark. He was born at Londonderry, New Hampshire, in 1728 and experienced Indian captivity in his boyhood. He knew the frontier country well and served with distinction in the French and Indian War. At the outbreak of the Revolutionary War, he received a colonel's commission and fought the British at Bunker Hill. He resigned from the army soon after this and formed an independent corps of men. When the British general Burgoyne sent a force into New Hampshire to collect supplies, Stark's men were there to provide opposition. In August 1777, the American and British forces clashed near Bennington, Vermont. Stark's forces won this battle. Burgoyne had to continue south without supplies and his army was defeated and captured at the Battle of Saratoga soon afterwards. This Battle of Saratoga is looked upon as one of the decisive battles of the Revolutionary War because the French agreed to ally themselves with the American forces after this victory. Congress appointed Stark a brigadier general and he served with distinction to the end of the war.

Colonel George Rogers Clark, a Scotch-Irishman, was commissioned in 1780 by Governor Patrick Henry of Virginia to organize and lead an expedition against certain British forts in the interior. Clark led the expedition overland in the winter months, and he and

George Rogers Clark, a military leader on the frontier, was never paid for his many years of valuable service. He died feeling that his countrymen were ungrateful.

his men suffered great physical hardships. The British were completely surprised, however, and the expedition redeemed the whole Northwest Territory for the American cause. His younger brother William, accompanied Meriwether Lewis on the famous Lewis and Clark expedition to the Northwest in 1806.

Another Scotch-Irishman was Henry Knox, who was born in Boston on July 25, 1750, of County Antrim stock. He fought the British at the Battle of Bunker Hill, was commissioned a colonel of the artillery, and served throughout the Revolutionary War, being advanced to major general in 1782. Knox later became Secretary of War in George Washington's first cabinet. He with-

Washington and His Cabinet: (left to right) George Washington; Henry Knox, Secretary of War; Alexander Hamilton, Secretary of Treasury; Thomas Jefferson, Secretary of State; and Edmund Randolph, Attorney General.

Anthony Wayne, hero of the Revolutionary War. Wayne's shrewd planning in the battle of Stony Point won him the title, "Mad Anthony."

drew from public life in 1794 after a long career and went to live on his farm in Maine.

Anthony Wayne, another leading general in the Revolutionary War, was born of Ulster parents in Pennsylvania. His greatest achievement was when he led his troops in the storming and capture of Stony Point on the Hudson River. One of the decisive American victories over the British took place at King's Mountain, North Carolina on October 7, 1780. The leader of the American forces was Colonel William Campbell whose family had immigrated to America from Ulster. Another American victory was won at the Battle of Cowpers, South Carolina, on January 17, 1781. A hero of

Battle of Fallen Timbers. In 1794, Wayne commanded troops on the frontier. His victory over the Indians at Fallen Timbers helped open land beyond the Ohio River to settlers.

this battle was Daniel Morgan, an elder of the Presbyterian Church, who was born in Ballinascreen, in County Derry. The leader of the American forces was Major Joseph McDowell, whose father had emigrated from Ulster. Other Scotch-Irish generals who served under Washington included William Thompson of Londonderry, William Irvine of Fermanagh, and Andrew Lewis of Donegal.

Among the most famous segments of the Continental Army was the "Pennsylvania Line." Seven companies of this regiment, the first, second, third, fourth, fifth, eighth, and ninth, were composed almost exclusively of Scotch-Irishmen. The sixth and seventh were composed mainly of Germans. Contemporary witnesses reported that these men were excellent marksmen and frequently able to hit targets far beyond the range of the ordinary musket. This is not too surprising. We know that most of the men on the frontier learned to use a rifle at a very early age, and their skill with "long rifles" was known among the Indians whom they had fought.

Scotch-Irish Presbyterians had no monopoly on patriotism during the Revolutionary War, but their synods took an early decisive stand against England, and a surprisingly large number of the leaders in the American Revolution were Presbyterians. It is true, however, that the Episcopalians, the Germans, and the Quakers would be less likely to want to fight England. The roots of the matter trace back to Ulster, and the quarrel with Britain which began in Ulster was continued in America by the Scotch-Irish who immigrated here. Their contribution to the cause of independence was considerable, especially in view of the fact that the Scotch-Irish in 1790 were only slightly over six percent of the total population of the United States. The census of 1790 stated that the population was 3,929,214. The Scotch-Irish, therefore, numbered only about 240,000 people.

PART VII.

The Political Influence of the Scots and Scotch-Irish in American History

The Scottish influence on the American political scene has been enormous. This is especially true when we realize that Scottish immigration has not been as large as many other groups. Many Scots held positions of importance in the colonial period of American history. Their influence continued during the American Revolution, the early years of the Republic, and down to modern times.

1. *The Founding of the United States*

Seven out of the 56 signers of the Declaration of Independence were Scots or Scotch-Irish. Two, Thomas McKean and John Hancock, were American-born. James Wilson and John Witherspoon had been born in Scotland. Three, James Smith, Matthew Thornton, and George Taylor had been born in Ulster. It is interesting to note that only seven of the entire group of signers were born abroad, and of these, five were Scots.

Nine of the first governors of the 13 newly created states, were Scots or Scotch-Irish: George Clinton of New York; Thomas McKean of Pennsylvania; William Livingston of New Jersey; Patrick Henry of Virginia; John MacKinley of Delaware; Richard

George Clinton was an officer in the American Revolution and governor of New York State.

John MacKinley was among nine of the first governors in the United States of Scottish or Scotch-Irish descent.

Caswell of North Carolina; John Rutledge of South Carolina; Archibald Bulloch of Georgia; Jonathan Trumbull of Connecticut. George Clinton of New York served in the Revolutionary War and was seven times elected governor of that state. He was also twice

John Rutledge of South Carolina served as a delegate to the Continental Congress, the Constitutional Convention, and as governor of his state.

Jonathan Trumbull served as governor of Connecticut for 15 years. During the Revolutionary War, he was one of Washington's valuable counselors.

John Blair of Virginia was a delegate to the Constitutional Convention and a Justice of the first United States Supreme Court.

elected Vice-President of the United States, and served in that office under Presidents Thomas Jefferson and James Madison. Clinton's father, Charles, who had been born in 1690 in County Longbord, Ireland, organized a group of colonists who came to America and settled in Ulster County, New York.

George Washington's cabinet included Alexander Hamilton, the Secretary of the Treasury, who was part Scottish. Many claim him as the greatest Secretary of the Treasury that this nation has ever had. Washington also appointed Henry Knox as Secretary of War and Edmund Randolph as Attorney General. The first Supreme Court included James Wilson and John Blair, both of whom were Scottish, and John Rutledge, an Ulster Scot.

2. *The Presidency*

Eleven of our nation's presidents have a Scottish or Scotch-Irish ancestry: James Monroe, Andrew Jackson, James K. Polk, James Buchanan, Andrew Johnson, Ulysses S. Grant, Chester Allan Arthur, Grover Cleveland, William McKinley, Woodrow Wilson, and Lyndon B. Johnson.

James Monroe

Andrew Jackson

The home of Andrew Jackson's parents is believed to have stood near Carrickfergus in Ulster.

James Monroe (1758-1831)

James Monroe became the fifth President of the United States of America in 1817. His family lived in the western sections of Virginia and included many Scottish and Welsh ancestors. He was just beginning his college work at William and Mary when the Revolutionary War broke out, and although he was ony 16 years of age at the time, he promptly joined the Continental Army. He served throughout the Revolutionary War, emerging with the rank of lieutenant colonel. In subsequent years he served in the Virginia Assembly, the Continental Congress, and the United States Senate. In addition, he represented the United States on missions to Spain, England, and France, served for several terms as the governor of Virginia, and held the offices of Secretary of State and Secretary of War.

President Monroe is probably best remembered for the foreign policy declaration bearing his name. The Monroe Doctrine was simply a statement made by the President. It declared that the nations of Europe should not interfere in the affairs of the western hemisphere. President Monroe was prompted to issue this declaration because several European nations were planning an invasion of Latin America to regain Spain's lost colonies, and the United States wanted to warn them against any such action.

Andrew Jackson (1767-1845)

Andrew Jackson, our seventh President, was the first who did not come from either the states of Virginia or Massachusetts. He was born in the back country of North Carolina and his parents were poor Scotch-Irish immigrants. Jackson's early life on the frontier had been harsh and severe. The reputation he gained during the War of 1812 by his victory over the British in the Battle of New Orleans made him a Presidential candidate in the election of 1824. Although he lost, the ground was well-prepared for his victory in 1828. The election of Jackson to the Presidency is sometimes referred to as a revolution. The people participated in that election as they never had before, and he was perhaps the first President to represent the people's choice in the true sense of the word.

James K. Polk (1795-1849)

James Knox Polk was the 11th President of the United States. The Polk family history dates back to the emigration of Robert Polk from Ulster in the late 17th century. His grandson, William, went to Pennsylvania, and his sons moved farther south to North Carolina. James Knox Polk was born at Mecklenburg, North Carolina, on November 2, 1795.

Polk sat in the House of Representatives from 1825 to 1839. He also served as governor of Tennessee. In 1844, he ran for President on the Democratic ticket with a pledge to secure the annexation of Texas and a settlement with Great Britain regarding the dispute over the Oregon country. The war with Mexico was fought during Polk's administration, and resulted in a large increase in the area of the United States. Many of the officers of the United States Army who fought in the Mexican War, such as General Winfield Scott, were also of Scottish descent.

James Buchanan (1791-1868)

James Buchanan, 15th President of the United States, was born near Mercersburg, Pennsylvania. His ancestors were Scotch-Irish Presbyterians. Buchanan served for 10 years in the House of Representatives, and then was sent by President Jackson to serve as Minister to Russia. He returned from Russia after two years at his post and entered the United States Senate where he served for two decades. He was Secretary of State under President Polk, minister to England under President Pierce, and then was elected President on the Democratic ticket in 1856.

Buchanan's term as President was filled with events of great historic importance. The Supreme Court handed down the Dred Scott decision regarding the status of Negro slaves in the territories, the Lincoln-Douglas debates were being carried on, and John Brown led the raid on the arsenal at Harper's Ferry. There have been few Presidents in the history of our country whose term in office have been as eventful as that of James Buchanan.

James K. Polk

James Buchanan

Andrew Johnson

Ulysses S. Grant

Grant's tomb in New York City.

Andrew Johnson (1808-1875)

Andrew Johnson of Tennessee was placed on the Republican ticket in 1864 as the Vice-Presidential nominee at the insistence of Abraham Lincoln, although he had opposed Lincoln in 1860. Johnson was a Southern Democrat who had remained loyal to the Union, and Lincoln wanted him on the ticket to promote the spirit of harmony when the war was over. Born in North Carolina, he had lived most of his life in the mountain country of eastern Tennessee, and it was here he made his political career.

His background included a condition of poverty equal to that of Lincoln; his father was a porter and his mother a maid. He mounted the ladder of politics step by step: mayor, member of the state legislature, member of Congress, governor, United States Senator, and finally Vice-President. When Lincoln was assassinated by John Wilkes Booth, Johnson became the 17th President of the United States. As a result of his conflicts with Congress, Johnson became the first and only President of the United States to be impeached. He was acquitted by one vote of the charge, and finished his term of office.

Ulysses S. Grant (1822-1885)

Ulysses S. Grant, our 18th President, was descended from a Matthew Grant who came to Massachusetts in 1630. He received an appointment to West Point in 1839, and served in the Mexican War, but resigned from the Army in 1854. Years of failure followed. When the Civil War broke out, Grant was making $50.00 a month as a clerk in a leather store owned by his two brothers at Galena, Illinois. He reentered the army as a colonel, but was soon raised to a brigadier general. His wartime record led to his being nominated for the Presidency by the Republican Party in 1868. Grant's brilliant record as an officer in the Civil War was not equaled by his two terms as President. Numerous scandals marred his administration, although he was never personally involved. He died in 1885, and is buried in a tomb monument in New York City, overlooking the Hudson River.

Chester A. Arthur (1830-1886)

Chester A. Arthur became the 21st President in 1881 when an assassin's bullet cut short the life of James Garfield. Arthur's ancestors, one of whom had been a Baptist clergyman, were from County Antrim in Northern Ireland. The new President had been a long-time member of the Republican organization. He championed civil service reform and bore himself with great dignity. He made a far better President than his critics had expected.

Grover Cleveland (1837-1908)

Grover Cleveland, the 22nd President, was elected in 1884. His father was a Presbyterian minister, and his mother the child of an Irish immigrant. He came up the hard way through the political paths of New York. He served as sheriff of Erie County, mayor of the city of Buffalo, and governor of the state. He was the champion of many reform measures and did all that he could as President to push for reforms on a national level. Cleveland is the only President who has served for two split terms, 1885-1889 and 1893-1897.

William McKinley (1843-1901)

William McKinley, whose ancestors were Scotch-Irish Presbyterians, became the 25th President of the United States. The election of 1896, in which he defeated the Democratic candidate, William J. Bryan, was one of the most controversial in American history. McKinley was President during the Spanish-American War. He made very few speeches and his success in political life was due mainly to the efforts of another Scotch-Irishman, Mark Hanna, the Cleveland industrialist, who managed his campaign and raised money on his behalf. President McKinley was assassinated while attending the Pan-American Exposition at Buffalo in 1901. Memorials to him have been erected at Canton, Ohio and Niles, Ohio.

Chester A. Arthur

Grover Cleveland

William McKinley

Woodrow Wilson

Lyndon B. Johnson

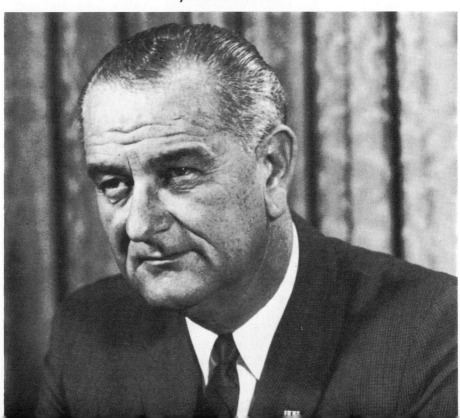

Woodrow Wilson (1856-1924)

Woodrow Wilson became the 28th President of the United States in 1913. He was a native of Staunton, Virginia, the first Southerner to serve as President since Andrew Johnson. His father was a Presbyterian minister, descended from James Wilson of Ulster who came to Philadelphia in 1807. Woodrow's mother, Jane Woodrow, was the daughter of a Scottish Presbyterian minister who emigrated to America in 1836. Wilson embarked upon a career in law but gave it up to become a college professor. He then advanced to the presidency of Princeton University and to the governorship of New Jersey. He became the Democratic nominee for President in 1912 and won the election due to the fact that the Republican Party had split and nominated two candidates.

The United States entered World War I in 1917 and President Wilson's dream was to see a league of nations in which all disputes would be settled before a war could start. He went to Paris in 1919 with the aim of establishing such an organization and was somewhat successful in his efforts. The United States Senate, however, refused to approve the Treaty of Versailles and so this country did not join the League of Nations. Some critics have claimed that Wilson's Scotch-Irish stubbornness cost him his dream and hold him personally responsible for the failure. Others claim that the Senate would not have approved the League even if Wilson had made some compromises. At any rate, Wilson died in 1924 without seeing his own country join the organization which he did so much to establish in the hope that it would ensure the cause of peace among the nations of the world.

Lyndon Baines Johnson (1908-   )

The story is reported that Samuel Ealy Johnson Sr., on August 27, 1908, announced the birth of Lyndon B. Johnson as follows, "A United States Senator was born this morning—my grandson." L. B. Johnson was born into a family that loved the game of politics. His father served five terms in the Texas legislature. Lyndon's grandmother, Eliza Bunton Johnson, was a niece of John Wheeler Bunton, a signer of the Texas declaration of independence. Eliza Johnson's cousin, Mary Desha, was a co-founder of the Daughters of the American Revolution. The Scottish ancestors of this family served for several generations in the Scottish parliament.

L. B. Johnson was elected to the House of Representatives in 1938 and to the Senate in 1948. In 1953 he became Minority Leader of the Democratic Party in the Senate. In 1960 he was elected Vice-President on the ticket with John F. Kennedy. Upon President Kennedy's assassination, Johnson assumed the Presidency. In 1964, he was elected President in his own right.

President Johnson is an extrovert who likes to talk and likes to have people around him. He has launched anti-poverty programs, anti-discrimination legislation, and many other measures since becoming President. He once summed up his philosophy as follows: "I am a freeman, an American, a U.S. Senator, and a Democrat, in that order. I am also a 'liberal,' a 'conservative,' a Texan, a taxpayer, a rancher, a businessman, a consumer, a parent, a voter, and not as young as I used to be or as old as I expect to be — and I am all those things in no fixed order."

3. *Statesmen of the 18th and 19th Centuries*

The list of Scot and Scotch-Irish cabinet members is truly remarkable. Of course, not all of these individuals are remembered as important figures in American history, but they were influential men in their times. Those who served as Secretary of State were Edward Livingston, Louis McLane, John Forsyth, John C. Calhoun, James Buchanan, Jeremiah S. Black, James G. Blaine, and John Hay. Out of this group emerged a President, James Buchanan, a Vice-President, John C. Calhoun, and a Presidential candidate, James G. Blaine. John Hay is probably best known for the so-called "Open Door" notes which he exchanged with various nations of the world in 1900.

Edward Livingston devised a modern code of reform and prison discipline.

John Hay was well-known in his time as a statesman and author.

John Bell of Tennessee ran unsuccessfully for President in 1860.

The men who served as Secretary of War included Henry Knox, James McHenry, John Armstrong, James Monroe, William Crawford, George Graham, John C. Calhoun, Peter Porter, John Bell, Jefferson Davis, Simon Cameron, and Alexander Ramsey. Jefferson Davis later became the president of the Confederacy and was the leader of the South throughout the Civil War.

As Secretary of the Treasury there were Alexander Hamilton, George W. Campbell, William Crawford, Louis McLane, Thomas Ewing, Thomas Corwin, James Guthrie, Howell Cobb, Salmon P. Chase, and Hugh McCulloch. Salmon P. Chase made a great contribution to the Civil War effort of the North by providing ways and means to finance the war.

Among the Secretaries of the Interior have been Thomas Ewing, Alexander H. H. Stuart, Robert McClelland, James Harlan, and Henry M. Teller. John McLean, James Campbell, Montgomery Blair, and Frank Hatton have served as Postmaster General.

Alexander Ramsey served as the second governor of the State of Minnesota.

Jefferson Davis was chosen president of the Confederacy in 1861.

Salmon P. Chase, a statesman, spent much of his life fighting slavery.

Montgomery Blair was active in Lincoln's campaign and served as Postmaster General in his cabinet.

John C. Calhoun believed that states could declare certain federal laws void within their boundaries.

James G. Blaine, a leading politician in the 19th century, held many positions during his career.

John C. Calhoun served his country in a variety of posts. He served as Secretary of War under President Monroe, Senator from South Carolina, and was elected Vice-President in 1824 and 1828. His disagreement with Andrew Jackson over the issue of states rights probably cost him a chance at the office of President. His keen mind and brilliant logic were respected by friend and foe alike. He died in 1850 after recommending that the South should withdraw from the Union because he felt that the North was growing so fast that the South would soon become a permanent minority with little to say respecting national policy.

James G. Blaine was a descendant of another James Blaine who emigrated from Londonderry in 1745. His paternal ancestors were mainly Scotch-Irish Presbyterians. The family first settled around Lancaster, Pennsylvania, but then moved over the mountains to the Pittsburgh area. After he married, Blaine made his home in Augusta, Maine. He was the Republican candidate for President in 1884. He also served as Secretary of State and was instrumental in the formation of the Pan-American Union.

Simon Cameron, born in Lancaster County, Pennsylvania, was of Scottish ancestry. He was Secretary of War during Abraham Lincoln's administration and Senator from Pennsylvania. Francis Preston Blair, journalist and politician, was descended from John Blair, a Scotch-Irishman who came to America in the early 18th century and settled in Bucks County, Pennsylvania. He held the first

Henry A. Wallace organized the Progressive party and ran unsuccessfully for President in 1948.

Simon Cameron of Pennsylvania held strong political control over this state for many years.

Stephen A. Douglas debated with Abraham Lincoln in a race for United States Senator and won the election.

chair of theology at Princeton. Francis Blair became editor of Andrew Jackson's party newspaper, *The Globe,* and from that time on was actively interested in politics. His son, Francis P. Blair, achieved fame as a general in the Civil War and in Missouri politics. Salmon Portland Chase was born at Cornish, New Hampshire, of Scottish ancestry. He was Secretary of the Treasury under Lincoln and Chief Justice of the Supreme Court for a number of years. Matthew Stanley Quay was born in Pennsylvania of Scotch-Irish ancestry. He was the political boss of Pennsylvania for many years, and served in the Senate from 1889 to his death in 1904.

John Breckenridge, and Stephen A. Douglas, Senator from Illinois, who were both candidates for President in 1860, were of Scottish descent. Douglas was born in Vermont and could trace his ancestry back to William Douglass, a Scot who came to Boston about the middle of the 17th century.

4. *Statesmen of the 20th Century*

Henry Agard Wallace was a distinguished plant geneticist who developed hybrid corn. This was a great contribution to American agriculture and increased the corn yield per acre many times. He was descended from Scotch-Irish ancestors and his grandfather had been a Presbyterian minister. President Franklin Delano Roosevelt appointed Wallace Secretary of Agriculture, in which position he was instrumental in drawing up much legislation designed to

Adlai Ewing Stevenson campaigned with Grover Cleveland and became Vice-President of the United States. Stevenson's son and grandson also became prominent in the world of politics.

help the farmer. In 1940, Wallace was Roosevelt's running mate and was elected Vice-President, but in 1944 he lost the nomination to Harry S. Truman.

Wallace then became Secretary of Commerce, but resigned in 1946. He ran for President on the Progressive Party ticket in 1948, but failed to carry even one state. He died in 1965.

Adlai Ewing Stevenson was another statesman from a family of statesmen. His grandfather, also named Adlai E. Stevenson, had been Vice-President of the United States under Grover Cleveland, and ran again for Vice-President in 1900, but was defeated. The

Adlai Stevenson, one of the outstanding men of the 20th century, was defeated in two presidential elections.

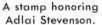

A stamp honoring
Adlai Stevenson.

Gale W. McGee, United States
Senator from Wyoming.

Tom McIntyre, United States
Senator from New Hampshire.

grandson was first called to Washington by President Franklin D. Roosevelt. Stevenson was later an American representative to the United Nations conference in 1945, and in 1948 he was elected governor of Illinois. In 1952 and 1956 he was the Democratic Party candidate for President of the United States, but lost to Dwight D. Eisenhower. President Kennedy appointed Stevenson United States Ambassador to the United Nations. He was serving in this position at the time of his death on July 19, 1965. His son Adlai Stevenson III is a member of the Illinois legislature, and embarked upon the beginning of a political career.

There are at least three members of Congress at the present time who are also of Scottish or Scotch-Irish descent: Senator Gale McGee of Wyoming, Senator Tom McIntyre of New Hampshire, and Senator George McGovern of South Dakota.

George McGovern,
United States Senator
from South Dakota.

PART VIII.

Scottish and Scotch-Irish Contributions to American Life

1. *Military Leaders*

The War of 1812

Mention has been made of the Scots who participated in the Revolutionary War. The War of 1812 went favorably for the Americans partly because of the actions of two men of Scottish ancestry in the United States Navy. Oliver Hazard Perry, born in Rhode Island, became one of the heroes of that war. Captain Perry was given the job of equipping a squadron and keeping the British from controlling Lake Erie. His fleet defeated the British squadron at Put-in-Bay in September 1813. This was a significant victory for the Americans, who had feared an invasion of their country by the British. Perry's short report to his immediate commander, General William Henry Harrison, has become quite famous: "We have met the enemy and they are ours: two ships, two brigs, one schooner, and one sloop."

Thomas McDonough, born in Delaware, entered the United States Navy and served in the Tripolitan War. He assisted Captain Stephen Decatur in the burning of the *Philadelphia*, a ship which the Tripolitan pirates had captured. During the War of 1812, McDonough was put in charge of the American squadron on Lake

Perry at the Battle of Lake Erie. During the battle, Perry's main ship was destroyed. However, Perry was rowed to another ship where he continued the battle until the British fleet had been defeated.

Champlain and had the task of keeping the British from invading the United States by that water route. He defeated the enemy squadron at the battle of Plattsburg on September 11, 1814. This naval victory, along with that of Perry's, ensured American control of the inland waterways. The British armies retreated to Canada and the country was safe from invasion from the north.

The War of 1812 ended with the signing of the Treaty of Ghent in December 1814. Unfortunately, communications were so slow that word did not reach the United States for several weeks. As a result, the famous Scotch-Irish frontier fighter and later President, Andrew Jackson, led his men in a battle with the British army, even though the war had been declared over.

Thomas Macdonough was awarded a gold medal by Congress for his important naval victory in the War of 1812.

Andrew Jackson at the Battle of New Orleans. Jackson defeated the British, not knowing the war was already over!

The Battle of New Orleans, painted by P. L. Debuccoup. Jackson's brilliant victory proved that the strength of the American Army was underestimated and restored the American people's faith in their fighting force.

Sir Edward Pakenham, the British commander, landed an army at New Orleans with the intention of capturing the city. General Jackson, fresh from his victory over the Creek Indians at Horseshoe Bend, stationed his Kentucky and Tennessee riflemen behind cotton bales to defend the city. The British soldiers attacked across open ground and were cut down in large numbers. General Pakenham was killed, and the British suffered nearly 2,000 casualties. The Americans lost only 13 men. The British expedition withdrew in defeat and Andrew Jackson became the hero of the hour. It was ironic, however, that the battle was fought in January 1815, while the peace treaty had been signed the previous month.

The War for Texan Independence

David Crockett was born in Hawkins County, Tennessee, an area which was heavily Scotch-Irish. His father fought in the battle of King's Mountain in the American Revolution. Crockett became widely known as a frontiersman and lost his life helping the Texans defend the Alamo in 1836.

Samuel Houston, soldier and statesman, was born in Rockridge County, Virginia. His paternal ancestors were Ulster Scots who

Sam Houston led Texas in the struggle for independence from Mexico.

David Crockett, frontiersman and politician, lost his life at the Alamo.

had migrated to Pennsylvania and later to Virginia in the first part of the 18th century. He served under Andrew Jackson during the War of 1812, and was wounded at the Battle of Horseshoe Bend on March 28, 1814.

Houston led the Texan forces when they defeated the army of General Santa Anna at the Battle of San Jacinto on April 21, 1836. Texas won its independence as a result of this battle, and Houston became the first President of the Texas Republic on October 22, 1836. He served as Senator after Texas was annexed to the United States in 1845, and in the 1850's he was elected governor of the state. He lost this position when he opposed secession from the Union.

A special postage stamp issued to commemorate Texas independence and honor Texas leaders, Sam Houston and Stephen F. Austin. A stamp (right) honoring Sam Houston.

The Civil War

Many individuals of Scottish descent served with distinction in the American Civil War. On the Union side were Generals Grant, McClellan, Hancock, McDowell, Rawlins, and Reynolds.

General Ulysses S. Grant was an officer on the western front in the early years of the Civil War. His greatest achievement during that period was the seige and capture of Vicksburg. Lincoln ordered him East to take charge of the Union armies after General Meade failed to follow up the victory over Lee at Gettysburg.

Grant continued to attack Lee, but only at a terrible loss in Union troops. Lincoln resisted the pressures that were put upon him to remove Grant, saying that he was the first Union general who seemed to keep the Union armies moving after Lee and the Confederates.

His determination and aggressiveness paid off and Lee was forced to retreat towards Richmond in 1865. When Lee's lines were threatened near Richmond, he moved his armies west hoping to join forces with another Confederate army. Grant moved ahead of him, however, and Lee was forced to surrender to Grant at Appomattox Court House, Virginia, on April 9, 1865.

General George Brinton McClellan had ancestors who came from Scotland to the United States early in the 18th century. His great grandfather, Samuel McClellan, served in the Revolutionary

George B. McClellan, soldier and engineer, ran for President in 1864.

W. S. Hancock (seated), ran unsuccessfully for President in 1880.

Irwin McDowell (center, facing left), commanded Union troops at Bull Run.

War. McClellan entered West Point in 1842, and was in command of the Army of the Potomac at the start of the Civil War. His armies met those of Lee in two important battles, the Peninsular Campaign and Antietam. Lee once was said to have remarked that McClellan was the best Union general that he ever faced. McClellan ran for the office of President on the Democratic ticket in 1864 and was defeated by Lincoln.

General Winfield Scott Hancock was named after one of the heroes of the Mexican War. He entered West Point in 1844, and some of his contemporaries there were Grant, McClellan, Reynolds, Rosecrans, Longstreet, Pickett, and Jackson. General Hancock served with distinction at Gettysburg. On the second day of that battle it was Hancock commanding the left wing who turned Lee's attack. On July 3, Hancock's corps was in the center of the Union lines and helped turn back the attack by Pickett's men.

General Irvin McDowell, a graduate of West Point in 1838, served with honor in the Mexican War. It was his misfortune, however, to be put in charge of the Union army at the First Battle of Bull Run. The Union forces retreated in confusion, and since McDowell had never had an independent command before, he was unable to restore order. General John A. Rawlins was the principal staff officer to General Grant throughout the Civil War. General John F. Reynolds graduated from West Point in 1841, fought in the Mexican War, and was killed by a Confederate sharpshooter at Gettysburg on July 1, 1863. A monument stands at Gettysburg on the spot where he fell.

Many of the officers serving the Confederacy were also of Scottish descent. General Thomas Jonathan Jackson, a West Point graduate, served in the Mexican War and taught at the Virginia Military Institute. His forces participated in the First Battle of Bull Run. "There is Jackson standing like a stone wall," a remark attributed to Brigadier General Barnard E. Bee, began the legend of "Stonewall" Jackson. General Jackson worked perfectly with Robert E. Lee, and together they inflicted many costly defeats on the

Thomas "Stonewall" Jackson was an outstanding Confederate commander.

Joseph E. Johnston won an important Confederate victory at Bull Run.

"Jeb" Stuart was a Confederate general noted for his bravery.

Union armies. He was shot by one of his own men on May 2, 1863, when returning to the lines. His loss was a great blow to General Lee and the South.

General Joseph E. Johnston, whose father had served in the Revolutionary War, entered West Point in 1825, participated in the Mexican War, and commanded some of the Confederate force at the First Battle of Bull Run. He was not one of the better Confederate generals. General James Ewell Brown Stuart, however, was one of the South's finest officers. Known as "Jeb," he became the "eyes" and "ears" of General Lee through his scouting expeditions. He was wounded in action on May 11, 1864 and died the following day. A statue of him stands in the city of Richmond, Virginia.

World War I and II

Among our modern military leaders was General Douglas MacArthur, who was enormously proud of his Scottish ancestors. His grandfather came to America in 1825, and rose to be governor of Wisconsin and a United States judge. His father was General Arthur MacArthur, who served in the Union Army during the Civil War and was a colonel at the age of 20. He later became the military-governor of the Philippine Islands. Douglas MacArthur grew up on Army frontier posts. He went to West Point and graduated first in his class in 1903. During World War I, he became a brigadier general and was wounded in action. In the 1930's he served in the Philippine Islands and was engaged in strengthening their army when the Japanese attacked Pearl Harbor in 1941.

MacArthur directed the defense of Bataan, and left only upon President Roosevelt's orders. An especially dramatic moment arrived in 1944 when MacArthur returned to the Philippines, as he promised that he would. President Truman appointed Mac-Arthur Supreme Commander of the Allied Occupation Forces in Japan. His success in rebuilding Japan while it was an occupied nation was an achievement almost equal to his conduct of the war.

General Douglas MacArthur commanded armies in the Pacific during World War II and supervised the reconstruction of Japan after the war. He also served as commander of United Nations forces in Korea until 1951. He died in 1964.

2. Inventors and Scientists

Scottish and Scotch-Irish representatives in the field of invention are numerous. Robert Fulton became famous by applying the steam engine to navigation. He was aided in this by Chancellor Livingston, also a Scot.

They built the first steamboat, the *Clermont*. In 1807 the *Clermont* successfully navigated the Hudson River by means of steam power and a new age began in water transportation.

The invention of the reaper, a machine which worked a revolution in American agriculture, was the work of Cyrus McCormick.

Asa Gray, a famous botanist of Scotch-Irish parentage, became one of the main defenders of Charles Darwin in America. John Muir, the noted American naturalist and conservationist, was born in Scotland. William Maclure has been referred to as the "father of American geology," and Alexander Wilson was a distinguished authority on birds.

The first public testing of McCormick's reaper in 1831.

John Muir, naturalist and writer, helped establish national parks.

Robert Fulton developed the first steamboat, the *Clermont*, with the help of Chancellor Livingston.

3. *Writers, Artists, and Musicians*

Among the Scottish representatives in the field of literature is Washington Irving, the son of a deacon and Scot Covenanter. Irving, born in New York City, published a famous series about life along the Hudson River known as the *Sketch Book*. One of the best known of these stories is that of Rip Van Winkle. Among his other works are *A Tour of the Prairies* and *The Conquest of Granada*.

Edgar Allen Poe, the poet and short story writer, was Scotch-Irish on his father's side. William James, philosopher and psychologist, was one of the main figures in the pragmatic school of American philosophy and author of *The Varieties of Religious Experience*. Henry James was a well-known novelist. Both of these men were of Scotch-Irish Presbyterian ancestry.

Washington Irving　　　　**William James**　　　　**Henry James**

Stephen Foster wrote many of his songs for traveling minstrel shows.

George Inness was a leading American landscape painter of the 1800's.

Edward MacDowell composed classical music for piano and orchestra.

Edwin Forrest was the earliest American born actor of first rank. He had a remarkably successful career both in the United States and in Europe. He became a wealthy man as a result, and when he died he willed nearly his entire estate as a home for aged actors, the Forrest Home in Philadelphia.

George Inness became one of the leading landscape painters in America, and his works can be found in most of the major art museums in America today. Thomas Eakins, whose paternal grandfather came to America from Northern Ireland, was also an outstanding painter and art teacher. Thomas Hart Benton, whose grandfather was a Senator from Missouri, is a prominent contemporary painter.

Stephen Collins Foster, whose family settled near Lancaster, Pennsylvania, was descended on both sides from Scotch-Irish emigrants. Foster gained a permanent place in American music by composing folk songs that appealed to a wide audience. Among his more popular compositions were *The Old Folks at Home, Oh, Susanna, My Old Kentucky Home, Jeanie with the Light Brown Hair,* and *Old Black Joe.* He spent his last years in poverty and obscurity and died in 1860, after a short illness in the charity ward of the Bellevue Hospital in New York City.

Edward Alexander MacDowell, another distinguished composer, was born in New York City, and was of Scottish ancestry. He wrote works of a classical nature and spent much of his time

James Gordon Bennett was founder and editor of the *New York Herald*.

A stamp issued in honor of **Horace Greeley,** journalist and politician.

touring Europe and America. Some of his compositions were *Woodland Sketches, Indian Suite,* and *Sea Pieces.*

4. *Journalists and Educators*

The first newspaper printed in America, the *Boston News-Letter,* was the work of a Scot named John Campbell. Other prominent journalists have been James Gordon Bennett, Horace Greeley, Henry W. Grady, and Whitelaw Reid. James Gordon Bennett worked his way up through the positions on the *New York Herald,* a family newspaper. He was responsible for sending Henry M. Stanley to Africa in 1870 to search for Dr. David Livingstone.

Horace Greeley went into journalism at an early age and made the *New York Tribune* one of the leading papers of the day. Greeley was not only well-known as a journalist, but he became involved in most of the leading reform movements of that period. He addressed an editorial open-letter to Abraham Lincoln in 1862, known as the "Prayer of Twenty Millions," in which he asked Lincoln to take a stand on the issue of slavery. He ran for President on the Democratic ticket in 1872 but was defeated and died soon afterwards. Whitelaw Reid served on the staff of the *Tribune* under Greeley, and upon the latter's death became editor-in-chief. After a successful career in journalism, he became a diplomat and served as minister to France and ambassador to Great Britain. Henry Woodfin Grady, a vigorous advocate of the so-called "New South"

Robert McCormick was an editor, publisher, and author of several books.

Tribune Tower in Chicago, was completed in 1925.

after the Civil War, was also a journalist of Scotch-Irish ancestry.

One of the more recent journalists of Scottish ancestry was Colonel Robert R. McCormick, publisher of the *Chicago Tribune*. His father had been ambassador to Austria-Hungary, Russia, and France, and the son grew up around the world. He studied law, but turned to journalism, and was probably the most controversial publisher of his time. When McCormick died on April 1, 1955, tributes came from many individuals, one of them being a fellow Scot, General Douglas MacArthur. President Eisenhower spoke of the death of McCormick and Joseph Pulitzer, who had died the day before, and said that in their passing "American journalism had lost the services of two of its outstanding publishers."

William Holmes McGuffey, educator and compiler of school-readers, was born in Washington County, Pennsylvania, but the family then settled near Youngstown, Ohio in 1802. He graduated from Washington College in 1826, and became a professor and then president of several colleges and universities. His fame, however, rests on his *Eclectic Readers* for elementary schools. While he was a professor at Miami University in Ohio, he began a series of schoolbooks. He wrote six of these in all and they went through many editions, reaching the fabulous sale of 122 million copies. These readers had great moral and cultural influence on the children of the 19th century.

Gilbert Highet   Kenneth Galbraith

Two contemporary educators of Scottish extraction are Gilbert Highet and John Kenneth Galbraith. Dr. Highet, Chairman of the department of Greek and Latin at Columbia University was born in Glasgow, Scotland. Dr. Galbraith was born in Ontario, an area where many Highlanders settled after immigrating to Canada.

5. *Businessmen and Trade Unionists*

The Scots have made numerous contributions to the field of business in America. Marcus Alonzo Hanna, a wealthy Cleveland industrialist, had Scotch-Irish ancestors. He was elected to the Senate from Ohio in 1897. Philip Danforth Armour, another Scotch-Irishman, made a fortune as a meat-packer and grain dealer. He went into the meat-packing business after the Civil War, and moved to Chicago just as that town was becoming the leading pork-packing center of the nation. Armour was one of the first to see the possibilities of the refrigerated car. Another businessman and banker of note was Andrew Mellon. He served as Secretary of the Treasury under Presidents Harding, Coolidge, and Hoover.

Mark Hanna, a skillful politician, managed the campaign of McKinley.

Philip Danforth Armour founded the well-known Armour and Company.

One of our foremost modern labor leaders, Philip Murray, was of Scottish descent. He rose to the Vice-Presidency of the United Mine Workers of America, and then became President of the Congress of Industrial Organizations, in the period when that trade union organization was enrolling millions of workers in the mass production industries. Another Scottish trade unionist is Douglas Fraser, a director of the United Automobile Workers Union and the head of their Chrysler and American Motors department. He was born in Glasgow, Scotland.

Andrew W. Mellon helped the United States Government solve many financial problems in the 1920's.

Conclusion

The preceding pages have shown how a relatively small group of people have exercised a significant influence on our nation's history. Scottish immigration turned away from the United States at an early period, because of the Revolutionary War, but it later resumed. The Bureau of the Census lists 789,261 immigrants from Scotland between 1820 and 1962. The census of 1960 recorded 213,026 foreign-born Scots in America, and 454,646 persons whose parents, or at least one of them, were born in Scotland.

The number of Scotch-Irish in America cannot be definitely established. We know that they were only a small group, but there are no separate figures that record how many of them immigrated. In the colonial days, there were no regular immigration statistics. When records were established, the Scotch-Irish were included with other immigrants from Ireland. It was not until 1930 that separate lists were kept of immigrants from Ulster. The records of these immigrants do not, however, distinguish between the Ulster Irish and the Ulster Scots. Therefore, exact figures on the Ulster Scots are impossible to obtain. The census of 1960 only showed that there were then 68,083 persons living in the United States who had been born in Northern Ireland, and 186,726 persons whose parents had come from there.

Kilts and bagpipes are no longer seen except in parades, but the Scottish influence in America lives on. The Scots and Scotch-Irish played an historic role in moulding our country—on the frontier, on the battlefield, in political life, and in culture—and much of what the United States is today is owed to these people.

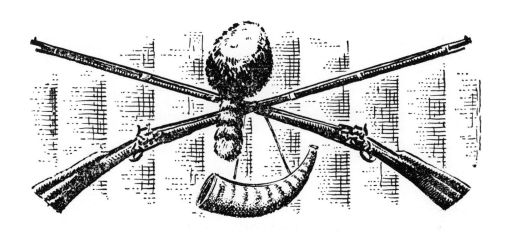

ACKNOWLEDGEMENTS

The illustrations are reproduced through the courtesy of: pp. 6, 12 (left), 14 (left and right), 15 (left), 16 (left and right), 26, 27, 30, 32, 35, 39 (top and bottom), 41, 42, 53 (bottom right), 57 (top and bottom left), 60 (center), 64 (bottom left and center), 66 (left and center), 70 (bottom left and right), 71, 73 (center and right), 77 (left), 78 (bottom center and right), 79 (right), 82 (top left and right), Independent Picture Service; pp. 11, 24 (left and right), 47 (top and bottom), 48 (top), 51 (top left and right and bottom left and right), 52, 53 (top and bottom left), 56 (top and bottom), 60 (top and bottom), 61 (top), 64 (top left, center, right, and bottom right), 65 (center and right), 67 (top), 70 (top), 72 (top left and right), 78 (bottom left), 79 (left and center), 80 (left), 83 (top left), Library of Congress; p. 12 (right), Independence National Historical Park Collection; pp. 15 (right), 48 (bottom), 65 (left), 66 (right), 68 (top left), 72 (bottom left and right), 77 (right), 78 (top), 80 (right), 83, Post Office Department, Division of Philately; p. 57 (bottom right), New York City Department of Parks; pp. 61 (bottom), 67 (bottom), Minnesota Democratic-Farmer-Labor Party; 68 (top center, right, and bottom), Office of the Senator; pp. 73 (left), 75 (left, center, right), National Archives; p. 76, United States Army; p. 81 (left and right), Chicago Tribune; p. 83 (top right), Armour and Company.

ABOUT THE AUTHOR . . .

JAMES E. JOHNSON was born in Johnson City, New York. After service in the Navy, he obtained his Bachelor of Arts Degree from the Triple Cities College of Syracuse University and his Master of Arts Degree from the University of Buffalo. In 1959, Syracuse University granted him a Doctor of Philosophy Degree in history. He is a member of the American Historical Association, the Organization of American Historians, and Phi Gamma Mu, the National Social Science Honor Society. Dr. Johnson taught United States history at Youngstown University and is now Professor of History at Bethel College, St. Paul, Minnesota.

The IN AMERICA *Series*

We specialize in publishing quality books for
young people. For a complete list please write:

LERNER PUBLICATIONS COMPANY
241 First Avenue North, Minneapolis, Minnesota 55401